UNLOCKING YOUR FULL POTENTIAL

A PATH TO INNER STRENGTH AND SUCCESS

DR. JAGADEESH PILLAI

|| Dedicated to all wisdom seekers around the world ||

᠈᠈᠈

Contents

Contents

Prayer

"Om Bhadram Karnebhih Shrunuyaama DevaahBhadram Pashyemaakshabhiryajatraah SthirairangaistushtuvaamsastanoobhihVyashema Devahitam YadaayuhSwasti Na Indro VridhashravaahSwasti Nah Pooshaa VishwavedaahSwasti Nastaarkshyo ArishtanemihSwasti No Brihaspatir DadhaatuOm Shantih, Shantih, Shantih"

The literal meaning of this mantra is: OM. O Gods! Let us hear auspicious words from our ears. O reverent Gods! Let us behold propitious visions from our eyes, let our organs and body be stable, healthy, and strong. Let us do that which is pleasing to the gods in the life span allotted to us. May Indra, inscribed in the scriptures, bring us fortune! May Pushan, the knower of the world, grant us prosperity! May Trakshya, who vanquishes enemies, bestow us with blessings! May Brihaspati bring us success!
OM Peace, Peace, Peace.

About The Author

Dr. Jagadeesh Pillai is a renowned Guinness World Record holder, writer, and researcher hailing from Varanasi, also known as the abode of Lord Shiva. With a Ph.D. in Vedic Science and a range of creative ideas and achievements, he is a true polymath. He is the author of more than 100 books including Research Publications. Although his roots can be traced back to Kerala, the people of Varanasi hold him in high regard and affectionately consider him one of their own.

In 1998, Dr. Pillai was offered a job at Banaras Hindu University, but he left the position after only two months to pursue greater goals in life. He believed that in order to study Indian scriptures and engage in other creative endeavours, he needed to retire from the daily grind of working solely for money at a young age.

He started an export business from scratch, using the knowledge he had gained from a previous job in the industry. His intelligence and unique approach to business led to great success in a short period of time, earning him more in just a decade and a half than he would have in a lifetime working in a government job. Upon the passing of Dr. APJ Abdul Kalam, Dr. Pillai decided to leave the business and dedicate himself to reading, studying, researching, and experimenting.

During his tenure in the export business, Dr. Pillai traveled to over 16 countries, gaining valuable insight and experiencing the world and life in detail.

Dr. Pillai has achieved four Guinness World Records in the following subjects:

"Script to Screen" - In this record, Dr. Pillai produced and directed an animation film within the shortest time possible, breaking the previous record set by Canadians. He has also received numerous national and international awards and recognitions for this achievement.

Longest Line of Postcards - For this record, Dr. Pillai created a line of 16,300 postcards on the occasion of the 163rd anniversary of Indian Postal Day. The event also included a questionnaire about the Indian flag.

Largest Poster Awareness Campaign - Dr. Pillai designed an awareness campaign on the subject of "Beti Bachao - Beti Padhao" (Save the Girl Child - Educate the Girl Child) to achieve this record.

Largest Envelope - In tribute to the Indian Prime Minister's "Make in India" initiative, Dr. Pillai created a 4000 square meter envelope using waste paper to achieve this record.

Attempted - **70000 Candles on a 210 kg Cake** - To celebrate the 70th Indian Independence Day, Dr. Pillai attempted to light 70,000 candles on a 210 kg cake, which was recorded in World Records India.

Attempted - **Documentary on Dhamek Stupa of Sarnath in 17 Languages** - Dr. Pillai attempted to create a documentary on the Dhamek Stupa of Sarnath, dubbing it in 17 different languages. The result of this attempt is currently awaiting confirmation from the Guinness World Records.

Dr. Pillai is skilled in teaching the Bhagavad Gita, a Hindu scripture, and is popular among young people. He has helped many young people improve their lives through his motivational teachings.

In addition to teaching, he has composed and sung numerous Sanskrit Bhajans and patriotic songs.

He has also written and directed several short films and documentaries for awareness campaigns, and has volunteered with the police in both UP and Kerala to spread awareness about various issues through videos and photography.

Incredibly, he has produced and directed over 100 documentaries about the city of Varanasi, all on his own.

He has also helped and guided more than 25 boys and girls to achieve world records through creative and innovative methods. He is a multifaceted person who uses his intellect and the blessings given to him by God to excel in various areas. He is both a teacher and a student, always learning and teaching, and is able to master any subject he comes across.

He is a selfless social activist and motivational speaker who has overcome struggles and failures to become a successful and enthusiastic individual with a rich life experience.

In addition to his work with the Bhagavad Gita, he is also an efficient Tarot card reader, Astro-Vastu consultant, and a talented singer and composer. He has sung the entire Ram Charita Manas and Bhagavad Gita in his own compositions, and has sung the phrase "Lokah Samastha Sukhino Bhavantu" in 50 different languages. He is currently working on a detailed and scientific study of Vedas, Upanishads, Puranas, and the Bhagavad Gita. He has also composed and sung the Hanuman Chalisa and Gayatri Mantra in 108 and 1008 different compositions, respectively.

Awards - Four Times Guinness World Records, Winner of Mahatma Gandhi Vishwa Shanti Puraskar, Mahatma Gandhi Global Peace Ambassador, Kashi Ratna Award, Dr. APJ Abdul Kalam Motivational Person of the Year 2017, Mother Teresa Award, Indira Gandhi Priyadarshini Award, Bharat Vikas Ratna Award, Udyog Ratna Award, Vigyan Prasar Award, Poorvanchal Ratn Samman.

ᐁᐁᐁ

Preface

In this book, Secrets to Find Your Inner Strength: A Guide to Achieving Your Goals, readers will discover the power of their inner strength and how to use it to reach their goals. Through this book, readers will learn how to identify their strengths, develop a plan to reach their goals, and stay motivated to achieve success.

This book is designed to help readers unlock their inner strength and use it to reach their goals. It provides practical advice and strategies to help readers identify their strengths, develop a plan to reach their goals, and stay motivated to achieve success. It also offers inspiring stories of people who have used their inner strength to reach their goals.

This book is for anyone who wants to unlock their inner strength and use it to reach their goals. It is for those who want to learn how to identify their strengths, develop a plan to reach their goals, and stay motivated to achieve success. It is also for those who want to be inspired by stories of people who have used their inner strength to reach their goals.

This book is an invaluable resource for anyone looking to unlock their inner strength and use it to reach their goals. It provides practical advice and strategies to help readers identify their strengths, develop a plan to reach their goals, and stay motivated to achieve success. It also offers inspiring stories of people who have used their inner strength to reach their goals. With this book, readers will gain the knowledge and confidence to unlock their inner strength and use it to reach their goals.

❦❦❦

ONE

Understanding Yourself and Your Goals

It is essential to understand yourself and your goals in order to achieve success. Knowing who you are and what you want to accomplish will help you stay focused and motivated.

The first step to understanding yourself is to identify your strengths and weaknesses. Take some time to reflect on your skills, talents, and abilities. Consider what you are good at and what you need to work on. This will help you determine what areas you need to focus on in order to reach your goals.

The next step is to set realistic goals. Think about what you want to achieve and how you plan to get there. Make sure your goals are achievable and measurable. Break down your goals into smaller, more manageable tasks. This will help you stay on track and make progress towards your goals.

Once you have identified your strengths and weaknesses and set realistic goals, it is important to create a plan of action. This plan should include specific steps you need to take in order to reach your goals. Make sure to include deadlines and milestones to help you stay on track.

Finally, it is important to stay motivated and focused. Remind yourself of why you are working towards your goals and what you will gain from achieving them. Celebrate your successes and learn from your mistakes.

Understanding yourself and your goals is essential to achieving success. By taking the time to identify your strengths and weaknesses, set realistic goals, create a plan of action, and stay motivated, you will be well on your way to achieving your goals and unlocking your inner strength.

ppp

"Success is not final, failure is not fatal: it is
the courage to continue that counts."

- Winston Churchill

❥❥❥

TWO

Identifying and Understanding Your Strengths and Weaknesses

It is important to recognize that everyone has both strengths and weaknesses, and that understanding them is the key to unlocking your inner strength.

The first step in understanding your strengths and weaknesses is to take an honest look at yourself. Ask yourself questions such as: What do I excel at? What do I struggle with? What do I enjoy doing? What do I find difficult? Taking the time to reflect on these questions can help you gain insight into your strengths and weaknesses.

Once you have identified your strengths and weaknesses, it is important to understand how they can help or hinder you in achieving your goals. Your strengths can be used to your advantage, while your weaknesses can be addressed and improved upon. For example, if you are a great communicator, you can use this strength to build relationships and network with others. On the other hand, if you struggle with organization, you can work on developing strategies to help you stay organized.

It is also important to recognize that your strengths and weaknesses can change over time. As you grow and develop, you may find that some of your strengths become weaknesses and vice versa. It is important to stay open to change and be willing to adjust your strategies accordingly.

Finally, it is important to remember that everyone has strengths and weaknesses. It is important to be kind to yourself and recognize that you are capable of achieving your goals, even if you have weaknesses. With the right strategies and a positive attitude, you can use your strengths and weaknesses to your advantage and unlock your inner strength.

ppp

"The only way to achieve the impossible is to believe it is possible."

- Charles Kingsleigh

❥❥❥

THREE

Setting and Prioritizing Goals and Objectives

Setting and achieving goals is a key component of finding your inner strength and achieving success. Goals provide direction and motivation, and help you stay focused on the path to success. Prioritizing your goals is essential to ensure that you are making progress and staying on track.

When setting goals, it is important to be realistic and to set achievable goals. Start by breaking down your goals into smaller, more manageable steps. This will help you stay focused and motivated. Additionally, it is important to set a timeline for each goal. This will help you stay on track and ensure that you are making progress.

Once you have set your goals, it is important to prioritize

them. This will help you focus on the most important goals first and ensure that you are making progress. Prioritizing your goals can be done in a variety of ways. You can prioritize by importance, by timeline, or by difficulty. Additionally, it is important to review your goals regularly to ensure that you are still on track.

When setting and prioritizing goals, it is important to remember to be flexible. Life can throw unexpected curveballs, and it is important to be able to adjust your goals accordingly. Additionally, it is important to celebrate your successes. Achieving goals can be difficult, and it is important to recognize and reward yourself for your hard work.

Setting and prioritizing goals is an essential part of finding your inner strength and achieving success. By breaking down your goals into smaller, more manageable steps, setting a timeline, and prioritizing your goals, you can stay focused and motivated on the path to success. Additionally, it is important to be flexible and to celebrate your successes. With the right approach, you can find your inner strength and achieve your goals.

❦❦❦

"*Success is not the key to happiness.
Happiness is the key to success. If you love
what you are doing, you will be successful.*"

- Albert Schweitzer

ϸϸϸ

FOUR

DEVELOPING SELF-AWARENESS AND SELF-CONFIDENCE

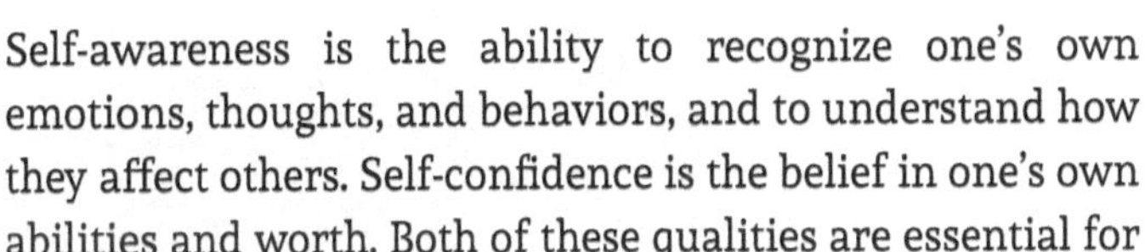

Self-awareness is the ability to recognize one's own emotions, thoughts, and behaviors, and to understand how they affect others. Self-confidence is the belief in one's own abilities and worth. Both of these qualities are essential for success in any endeavor.

Self-awareness is the foundation of self-confidence. It is important to understand one's strengths and weaknesses, and to be honest with oneself about them. This allows one to focus on areas that need improvement and to develop strategies to overcome any obstacles. Additionally, self-awareness helps one to recognize and accept their emotions, and to understand how they affect their behavior.

Self-confidence is the belief in one's own abilities and worth. It is important to recognize and celebrate successes, no matter how small. This helps to build self-confidence and encourages one to take risks and try new things. Additionally, it is important to be kind to oneself and to practice self-compassion. This means being gentle and understanding with oneself, and not being too hard on oneself when mistakes are made.

Developing self-awareness and self-confidence can be a difficult process, but it is essential for achieving one's goals. It is important to take the time to reflect on one's thoughts and feelings, and to be honest with oneself about one's strengths and weaknesses. Additionally, it is important to recognize and celebrate successes, and to practice self-compassion. With self-awareness and self-confidence, one can take risks and try new things, and ultimately achieve their goals.

ഗഗഗ

"Success is not a destination, it is a journey."

- Zig Ziglar

♥♥♥

FIVE

Cultivating Positive Attitudes and Mindset

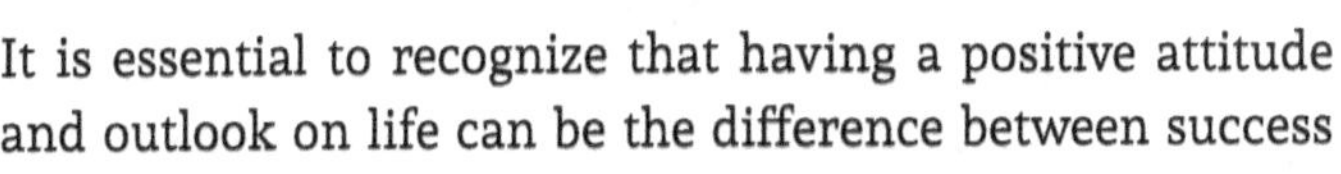

It is essential to recognize that having a positive attitude and outlook on life can be the difference between success and failure.

A positive attitude and mindset can be cultivated through a variety of methods. One of the most effective is to focus on the positive aspects of life and to be grateful for what one has. This can be done by writing down three things each day that one is grateful for, or by taking time to appreciate the beauty of nature. Additionally, it is important to practice self-care and to take time to relax and enjoy life.

Another way to cultivate a positive attitude and mindset is to surround oneself with positive people. This can be done by joining a support group or by engaging in activities with friends and family who have a positive outlook on life. Additionally, it is important to practice positive self-talk and to focus on the good in life rather than the bad.

Finally, it is important to set realistic goals and to take small steps towards achieving them. This can be done by breaking down larger goals into smaller, more manageable tasks. Additionally, it is important to celebrate successes, no matter how small, and to use them as motivation to keep going.

Cultivating a positive attitude and mindset is essential for achieving one's goals. It is important to focus on the positive aspects of life, to practice self-care, to surround oneself with positive people, and to set realistic goals. By doing so, one can create an environment that is conducive to success and can help to unlock one's inner strength.

᠉᠉᠉

"Success is not a matter of luck, it is a matter of choice."

- William Jennings Bryan

❧❧❧

SIX

DEVELOPING COPING SKILLS AND RESILIENCE

Coping skills are the strategies and techniques we use to manage difficult emotions, thoughts, and behaviors. They help us to manage stress, anxiety, and other difficult emotions. Resilience is the ability to bounce back from adversity and to remain strong in the face of challenges.

Developing coping skills and resilience is essential for achieving one's goals. It helps us to stay focused and motivated, even when faced with obstacles. It also helps us to remain positive and to keep our eyes on the prize.

The first step in developing coping skills and resilience is to identify our triggers. Triggers are the events, people, or situations that cause us to feel overwhelmed or stressed. Once we have identified our triggers, we can begin to develop strategies to manage them. This may include deep breathing, mindfulness, or other relaxation techniques.

The next step is to develop a plan for dealing with difficult emotions. This may include journaling, talking to a friend, or engaging in a physical activity. It is important to remember that it is okay to feel overwhelmed or stressed. It is important to acknowledge these feelings and to take steps to manage them.

The third step is to practice self-care. Self-care is any activity that helps us to relax and recharge. This may include taking a hot bath, going for a walk, or engaging in a hobby. It is important to make time for self-care, as it can help us to stay focused and motivated.

Finally, it is important to practice gratitude. Gratitude helps us to stay positive and to appreciate the good things in our lives. It can also help us to stay focused on our goals and to remain resilient in the face of adversity.

Developing coping skills and resilience is essential for achieving one's goals. By identifying our triggers, developing a plan for managing them, and practicing self-care, we can increase our resilience and better handle life's challenges. Additionally, seeking support from friends, family, or a mental health professional can also help us build our coping skills and resilience.

ppp

"*Success is not a sprint, it is a marathon.*"

❥❥❥

SEVEN

Rediscovering and Rekindling Your Passions

The first step to rediscovering and rekindling your passions is to take a step back and reflect on what you truly enjoy. Think about the activities that bring you joy and make you feel alive. It could be anything from painting to playing a sport, or even something as simple as reading a book. Once you have identified your passions, it is important to make time for them. This could mean setting aside a few hours each week to dedicate to your passions, or even just a few minutes each day.

The next step is to find ways to make your passions more meaningful. This could involve exploring new ways to engage with your passions, such as joining a club or taking a class. It could also involve connecting with others who share your passions, as this can help to motivate and inspire you. Additionally, it is important to set goals for yourself and to track your progress. This will help to keep you motivated and will also provide a sense of accomplishment when you reach your goals.

Finally, it is important to remember that rediscovering and rekindling your passions is a journey. It is not something that can be achieved overnight, and it is important to be patient and kind to yourself. It is also important to remember that it is okay to take breaks and to give yourself time to rest and recharge.

Rediscovering and rekindling your passions can be a powerful and rewarding experience. By taking the time to reflect on what you enjoy, making time for your passions, and setting goals for yourself, you can unlock the secrets to finding your inner strength and achieving your goals.

ppp

"Success is not about how much you have, it
is about how much you give."

♥♥♥

EIGHT

DEVELOPING EFFECTIVE TIME MANAGEMENT STRATEGIES

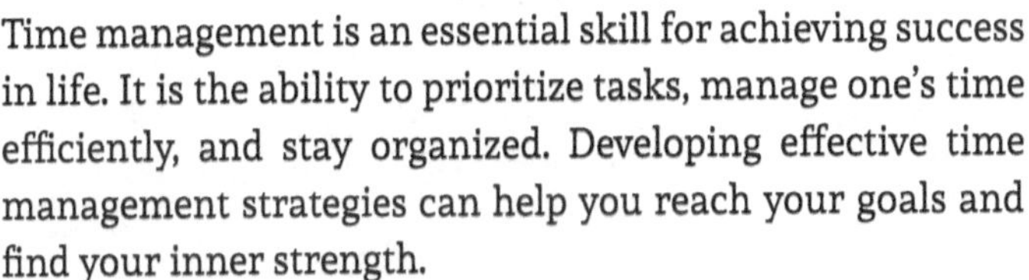

Time management is an essential skill for achieving success in life. It is the ability to prioritize tasks, manage one's time efficiently, and stay organized. Developing effective time management strategies can help you reach your goals and find your inner strength.

The first step in developing effective time management strategies is to identify your goals. What do you want to accomplish? What are your short-term and long-term goals? Once you have identified your goals, you can create a plan to achieve them.

The next step is to create a schedule. Make sure to include time for work, leisure, and rest. Prioritize tasks and set realistic deadlines. Break down large tasks into smaller, more manageable chunks. This will help you stay on track and avoid procrastination.

It is also important to practice self-discipline. Set boundaries and stick to them. Avoid distractions and stay focused on the task at hand. Make sure to take regular breaks to recharge and stay motivated.

Finally, it is important to be flexible. Life is unpredictable and things don't always go as planned. Be prepared to adjust your schedule and goals as needed.

Developing effective time management strategies can help you reach your goals and find your inner strength. Identify your goals, create a schedule, practice self-discipline, and be flexible. With these strategies, you can make the most of your time and achieve success.

ᚦᚦᚦ

Success is not a result of spontaneous combustion. You must set yourself on fire."

- Arnold H. Glasow

ϷϷϷ

NINE

Overcoming Fear and Releasing Stress

Fear and stress can be two of the most debilitating emotions that can prevent us from achieving our goals. In this chapter of Secrets to Find Your Inner Strength: A Guide to Achieving Your Goals, we will explore how to overcome fear and release stress in order to unlock our potential and reach our goals.

The first step to overcoming fear and releasing stress is to identify the source of the fear or stress. Is it a particular situation or person? Is it a fear of failure or success? Once the source is identified, it is important to understand why it is causing fear or stress. Is it a lack of confidence or a lack of knowledge?

The next step is to develop a plan to address the fear or stress. This could include seeking professional help, such as a therapist or coach, or it could include developing a plan of action to address the fear or stress. This could include setting achievable goals, developing a support system, or learning new skills.

Once a plan is in place, it is important to take action. This could include facing the fear or stress head-on, or it could include taking small steps to gradually reduce the fear or stress. It is important to remember that progress is not always linear, and it is okay to take a step back if needed.

Finally, it is important to practice self-care. This could include taking time for yourself, engaging in activities that bring joy, or simply taking a break from the fear or stress. It is important to remember that fear and stress can be overcome, and that it is possible to find inner strength and reach our goals.

By following these steps, we can learn to overcome fear and release stress in order to unlock our potential and reach our goals. With dedication and perseverance, we can find our inner strength and achieve our goals.

ᐅᐅᐅ

"*Success is not a straight line, it is a winding road.*"

♡♡♡

TEN

Establishing and Maintaining Healthy Habits

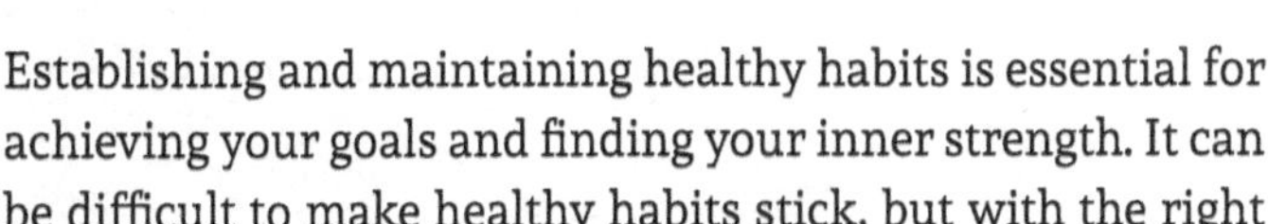

Establishing and maintaining healthy habits is essential for achieving your goals and finding your inner strength. It can be difficult to make healthy habits stick, but with the right strategies, you can make them part of your daily routine.

The first step to establishing healthy habits is to identify your goals. What do you want to achieve? What do you need to do to get there? Once you have identified your goals, you can create a plan to help you reach them. This plan should include specific steps that you can take each day to move closer to your goals.

Next, you need to create a schedule that will help you stick to your plan. This schedule should include time for exercise, healthy eating, and relaxation. Make sure to include activities that you enjoy, as this will make it easier to stick to your plan.

Once you have created a plan and a schedule, it is important to stay motivated. Find ways to reward yourself for sticking to your plan, such as taking a break or treating yourself to something special. Additionally, it is important to stay positive and remind yourself of why you are doing this.

Finally, it is important to be consistent. Make sure to stick to your plan and schedule, even when it is difficult. If you find yourself struggling, take a break and come back to it later.

Establishing and maintaining healthy habits is essential for achieving your goals and finding your inner strength. With the right strategies, you can make healthy habits part of your daily routine and move closer to your goals. By creating a plan, a schedule, staying motivated, and being consistent, you can make healthy habits stick and find your inner strength.

ᗡᗡᗡ

"*Success is not a matter of luck, it is a matter of hard work and dedication.*"

ᗷᗷᗷ

ELEVEN

UNDERSTANDING THE POWER OF MEDITATION

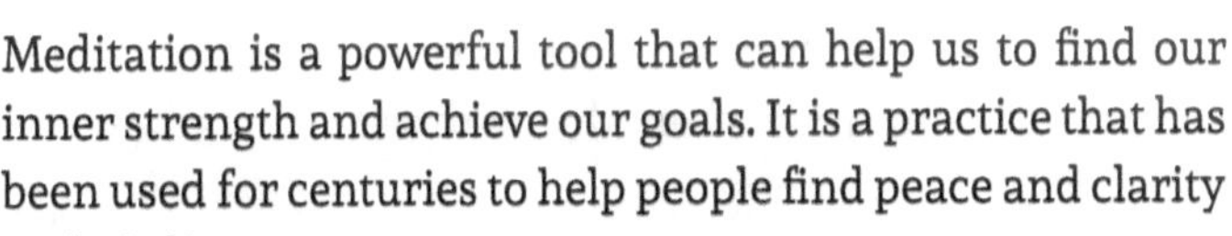

Meditation is a powerful tool that can help us to find our inner strength and achieve our goals. It is a practice that has been used for centuries to help people find peace and clarity in their lives.

Meditation can help us to become more mindful and aware of our thoughts and feelings. It can help us to become more present in the moment and to be more aware of our surroundings. It can also help us to become more aware of our inner strength and to tap into it.

When we meditate, we can focus on our breath and become more aware of our body and mind. We can become aware of our thoughts and feelings and how they affect us. We can also become aware of our inner strength and how it can help us to achieve our goals.

Meditation can help us to become more focused and to stay on track with our goals. It can help us to become more disciplined and to stay motivated. It can also help us to become more creative and to think outside the box.

Meditation can also help us to become more resilient and to cope with difficult situations. It can help us to become more compassionate and understanding of ourselves and others. It can also help us to become more confident and to trust our own decisions.

Meditation can be a powerful tool to help us find our inner strength and to achieve our goals. It can help us to become more mindful and aware of our thoughts and feelings. It can also help us to become more focused, disciplined, and creative. Finally, it can help us to become more resilient and compassionate. With regular practice, meditation can help us to unlock our inner strength and to reach our goals.

ႦႦႦ

"Success is not a destination, it is a process."

❥❥❥

TWELVE

EXPLORING MINDFUL LIVING AND LIVING IN THE MOMENT

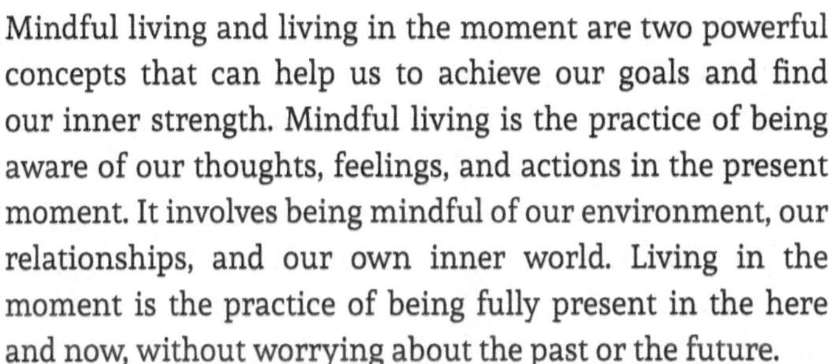

Mindful living and living in the moment are two powerful concepts that can help us to achieve our goals and find our inner strength. Mindful living is the practice of being aware of our thoughts, feelings, and actions in the present moment. It involves being mindful of our environment, our relationships, and our own inner world. Living in the moment is the practice of being fully present in the here and now, without worrying about the past or the future.

When we practice mindful living and living in the moment, we become more aware of our thoughts, feelings, and actions. We become more aware of our environment and our relationships. We become more aware of our own inner world and the power of our thoughts and feelings. We become more aware of our own potential and the power of our actions.

Mindful living and living in the moment can help us to achieve our goals and find our inner strength. When we practice mindful living, we become more aware of our thoughts and feelings, and we can use this awareness to make better decisions. We can use this awareness to make better choices and take better actions. When we practice living in the moment, we become more aware of our environment and our relationships, and we can use this awareness to create better relationships and a better environment.

Mindful living and living in the moment can also help us to find our inner strength. When we practice mindful living, we become more aware of our thoughts and feelings, and we can use this awareness to identify our strengths and weaknesses. We can use this awareness to build on our strengths and work on our weaknesses. When we practice living in the moment, we become more aware of our environment and our relationships, and we can use this awareness to create a supportive environment and build strong relationships.

Mindful living and living in the moment can help us to achieve our goals and find our inner strength. By being mindful of our thoughts, feelings, and actions, we can make better decisions, stay focused on our goals, and be more resilient in the face of setbacks and challenges. Mindfulness practices such as meditation, deep breathing, and gratitude can help us cultivate awareness and focus, reducing stress and promoting well-being. By living in the moment and focusing on the present, we can let go of past regrets and future worries, and fully engage in life's opportunities and challenges.

❧❧❧

"Success is not a one-time event, it is a lifestyle."

❥❥❥

THIRTEEN

ENGAGING IN SELF-REFLECTION FOR PERSONAL GROWTH

Engaging in self-reflection is an essential part of personal growth and achieving your goals. It is a process of examining your thoughts, feelings, and behaviors to gain insight into yourself and your life. Self-reflection can help you identify areas of your life that need improvement, as well as areas where you are succeeding. It can also help you gain clarity on your goals and how to reach them.

Self-reflection is a powerful tool for personal growth. It can help you become more aware of your strengths and weaknesses, and how to use them to your advantage. It can also help you identify areas of your life that need improvement, and how to go about making those changes. Self-reflection can also help you gain insight into your motivations and values, and how they influence your decisions and actions.

The process of self-reflection begins with taking the time to reflect on your thoughts, feelings, and behaviors. This can be done through journaling, meditation, or simply taking a few moments to sit and think. Once you have identified areas of your life that need improvement, you can begin to create a plan of action. This plan should include specific goals and steps to take to reach those goals.

In addition to creating a plan of action, self-reflection can also help you gain insight into yourself and your life. This can be done by asking yourself questions such as: What do I value most in life? What are my strengths and weaknesses? What do I need to do to reach my goals?

Engaging in self-reflection can be a difficult process, but it is essential for personal growth and achieving your goals. It can help you gain clarity on your goals and how to reach them, as well as provide insight into yourself and your life. By taking the time to reflect on your thoughts, feelings, and behaviors, you can create a plan of action and gain insight into yourself and your life. Self reflection can also lead to increased self-awareness and self-understanding, which can improve relationships and communication with others. Regular self-reflection can also help identify patterns and habits that may be hindering personal growth and success, and allow you to make changes towards a more fulfilling life. Additionally, self-reflection can increase gratitude and enhance overall well-being, helping to boost resilience and increase motivation towards achieving personal goals.

ᗞᗞᗞ

"Success is not a matter of luck, it is a matter
of perseverance and resilience."

ᑭᑭᑭ

FOURTEEN

DEVELOPING A SUPPORTIVE NETWORK OF PEOPLE

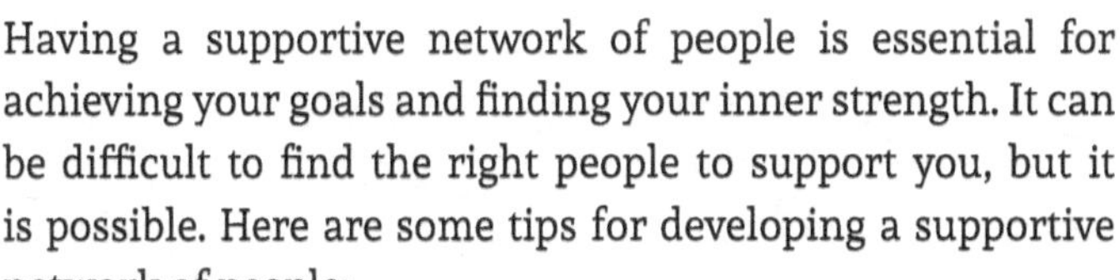

Having a supportive network of people is essential for achieving your goals and finding your inner strength. It can be difficult to find the right people to support you, but it is possible. Here are some tips for developing a supportive network of people:

1. Reach out to your family and friends. Your family and friends are the most likely people to be supportive of your goals and dreams. They know you best and can provide you with the encouragement and advice you need to stay motivated and on track.

2. Join a support group. Support groups are a great way to meet people who are going through similar experiences and can provide you with the emotional support you need.

3. Connect with mentors. Mentors can provide you with valuable advice and guidance. They can help you stay focused and motivated and provide you with the tools and resources you need to reach your goals.

4. Participate in online communities. Online communities are a great way to connect with people who share similar interests and goals. You can learn from each other and provide each other with the support and encouragement you need to stay on track.

5. Attend networking events. Networking events are a great way to meet new people and build relationships. You can learn from each other and build a strong network of people who can help you reach your goals.

Having a supportive network of people is essential for achieving your goals and finding your inner strength. With the right people in your corner, you can stay motivated and on track to reach your goals. By following these tips, you can develop a strong network of people who can provide you with the support and encouragement you need to reach your goals and find your inner strength.

ϷϷϷ

"Success is not a matter of chance, it is a matter of choice."

FIFTEEN

CELEBRATING ACHIEVEMENTS AND CREATING LASTING CHANGE

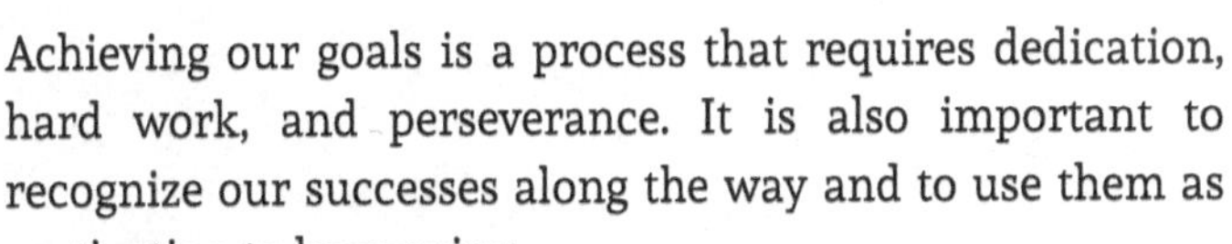

Achieving our goals is a process that requires dedication, hard work, and perseverance. It is also important to recognize our successes along the way and to use them as motivation to keep going.

Celebrating our achievements is a great way to recognize our progress and to stay motivated. It can be as simple as taking a few moments to reflect on our accomplishments and to appreciate the hard work we have put in. This can be done alone or with friends and family. Taking the time to recognize our successes can help us to stay focused and to keep striving for our goals.

Creating lasting change is also essential for achieving our

goals. This means making small, consistent changes in our lives that will help us to reach our goals. This could include setting aside time each day to work on our goals, creating a plan of action, and breaking down our goals into smaller, more manageable tasks. Making these changes can help us to stay on track and to stay motivated.

Finally, it is important to remember that achieving our goals is a journey. It is not something that happens overnight. It takes time, dedication, and hard work. Celebrating our achievements and creating lasting change can help us to stay focused and motivated on our journey.

By taking the time to recognize our successes and to make small, consistent changes in our lives, we can stay on track and reach our goals. Celebrating our achievements and creating lasting change can help us to stay motivated and to find our inner strength. With dedication and hard work, we can achieve our goals and find our inner strength.

ϷϷϷ

"Success is not a matter of luck, it is a matter
of courage and determination."

ϷϷϷ

Other Books Of The Author

1. The Moments When I Met God
2. Kashiyile Theertha Pathangal
3. GURU GYAN VANI
4. Abhiprerak Gita
5. ASSI SE JAIN GHAT TAK
6. Hopelessness of Arjuna
7. The Soul and It's True Nature
8. Sense of Action (Karma)
9. Action through Wisdom
10. Action through Wisdom
11. THEORY AND PRACTICAL OF EVERY ACTION
12. LOGICAL UNDERSTANDING OF THE SUPREME
13. THE IMPERISHABLE SUPREME
14. Yatra Nishadraj se Hanuman Ghat Tak
15. Yatra Karnatak Ghat se Raja Ghat Tak
16. Yatra Pandey Ghat se Prayagraj Ghat Tak
17. Yatra Ranjendra Prasad Ghat se Dattatreya Ghat Tak
18. YaatraSindhiya Ghat se Gwaliar Ghat Tak
19. Yatra Mangala Gauri Ghat se Hanuman Gadhi Ghat Tak
20. Yatra Gaay Ghat Se Nishad Ghat Tak
21. MAA GANGA, GHATEN EVM UTSAV
22. Ganga Arti Dev Deepavali evam Any Utsav
23. Potentials of Digitalized India
24. VEDIC CONSCIOUSNESS
25. A Brief Introduction to Vedic Science
26. Kashi ke Barah Jyotirling
27. IMPACT OF MOTIVATION
28. Let's have a Milky Way Journey
29. Color Therapy in a Nutshell

59. The Holistic Cow: A Look at the Physical, Spiritual, and Cultural Importance of Cows in India
60. Arts of Healing
61. Exploring the Divine
62. Understanding Five Elements
63. The Etymology of Ram
64. Symbols of India
65. Voice of Change (About Speeches of Great Men)
66. She Speaks (About Speeches of Great Women)
67. Patriotism on Celluloid – Brief About Patriotic Films
68. The Music of Motivation: A Brief Guide to Inspirational Film Songs
69. **Unlocking the Secrets of the Dashopanishads**
70. A Cultural Mosaic
71. Ancient Traditions, Modern Minds
72. Ecos of Ancient Wisdom
73. Beneath the Surface
74. From Temples to Ashrams
75. Sages of the Subcontinent
76. The Art of Healing (Ayurveda, Yoga & Naturopathy)
77. Indian Kitchen
78. The Festivals of India
79. The Indian Epics Retold
80. The Power of Mantras
81. The Indian River Ganges
82. The Indian Architecture
83. Rites of Passage
84. The Indian Silk Road
85. The Indian Literature
86. The Indian Villages
87. The Indian Folks & Crafts
88. The Way of Buddha
89. The Ramayan of Tulsidas

90. Astrological Remedies
91. The Secret Power of Motivation
92. Secret of Developing your Inner Strength
93. The Secret Path to Motivation
94. The Art and Secret of Positive Thinking
95. The Secrets of Practicing Ethical Living
96. Indian Art and Painting
97. The Indian Herbalism
98. Bharatanatyam to Kathak
99. Exploring India's Astrological Remedies
100. The Indian Festival of Flowers
101. Indian Handicrafts
102. The Splashes of Joy – India's Colour Festival
103. The Indian Science of Astrology
104. The Indian Mythology
105. Path to Enlightenment
106. The Indian Spirituality for Children
107. Aromas of India
108. The Secrets of Healthy Relationships
109. Ancestral Ties
110. The Indian Street Food
111. Discovering America
112. The Indian Textile
113. Listening to Motivational Speeches
114. Taste of India
115. A Cultural Journey through Indian Nuptials
116. Motivational Quote for Change
117. Secret Strategies for Making Money
118. Secrets to Cultivate a Positive Mindset
119. A Tapestry of Cultures: Exploring India from Kashmir to Kanyakumari
120. Achieving Your Dreams with Resilience: Secret Strategies for Overcoming Obstacles

ppp

Contact

DR. JAGADEESH PILLAI

MBA & PhD in Vedic Science

Four Times Guinness World Record Holder

Winner of Mahatma Gandhi Vishwa Shanti Puraskar and
Global Peace Ambassador

Gemology, Astro & Vastu Consultant - Spiritual Counselor

Consultant for designing World Record Ideas

Efficient Tarot Card Reader

9839093003

myrichindia@gmail.com

drjagadeeshpillai@facebook

drjagadeeshpillai@instagram
jagadeeshpillai@youtube

www. JAGADEESHPILLAI.com

༄༄༄

|| LOKAHA SAMASTHAHA SUKHINO BHAVANTU ||

❧❧❧